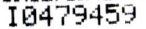

Table Of Contents

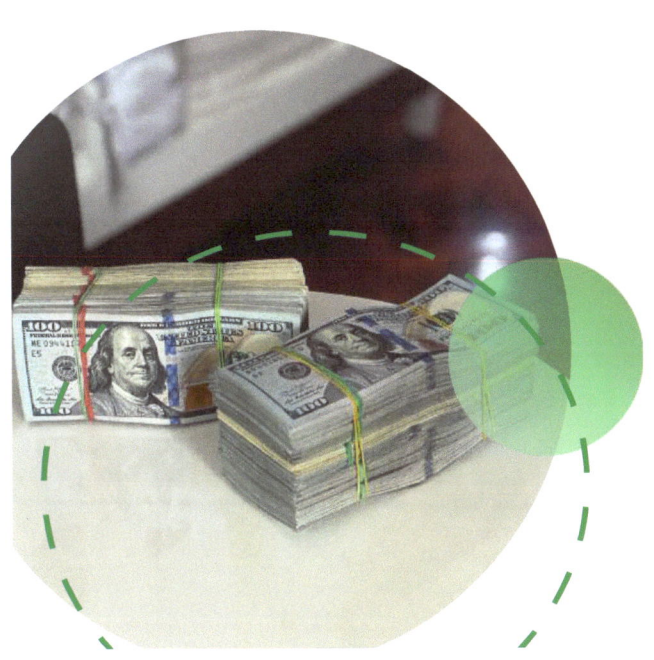

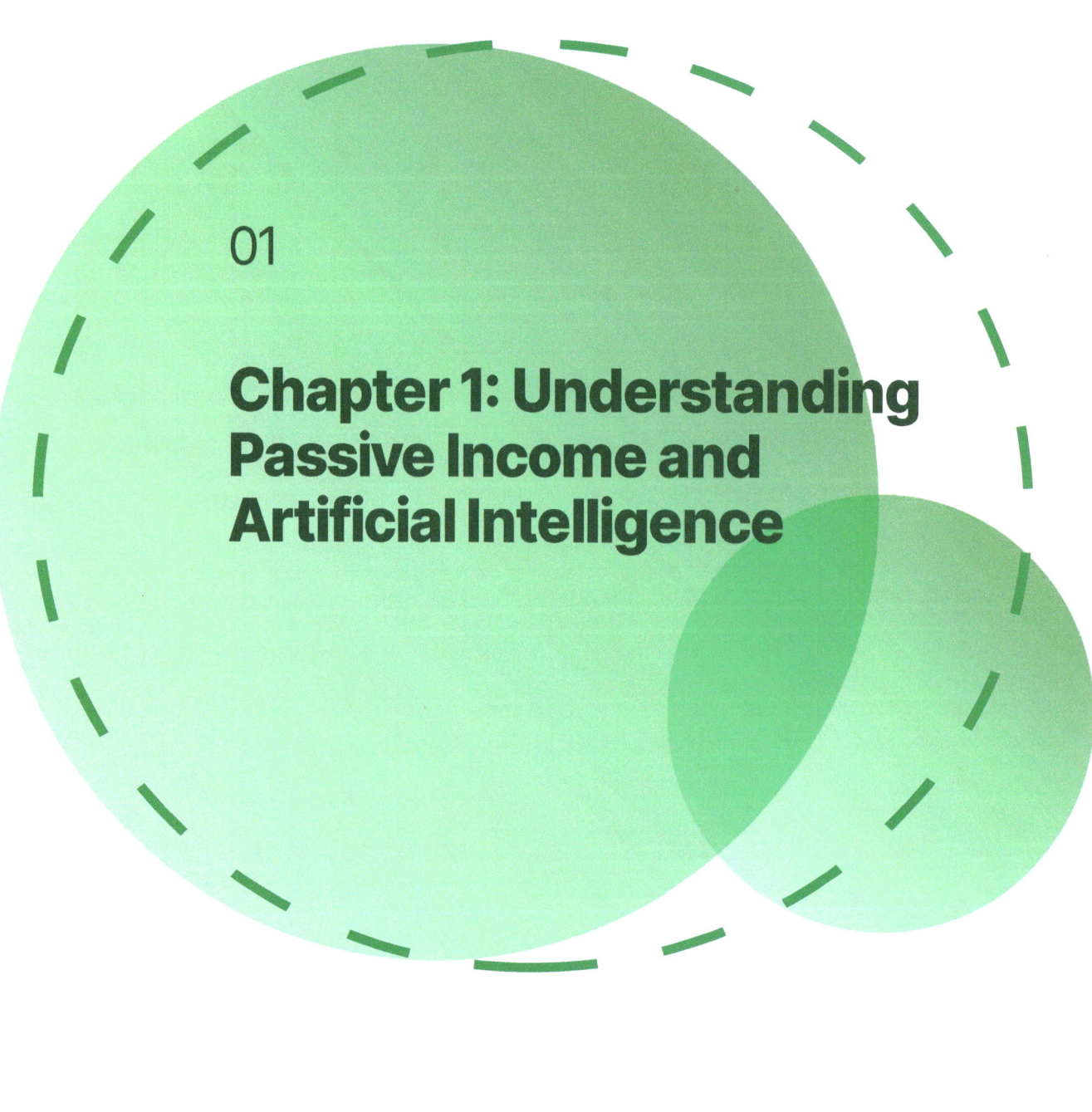

01

Chapter 1: Understanding Passive Income and Artificial Intelligence

The Basics of Passive Income

In this subchapter, we will delve into the basics of passive income and how artificial intelligence can play a significant role in helping you achieve financial freedom. Passive income is money earned with little to no effort on your part, making it an attractive option for those looking to increase their wealth without actively working for it. By harnessing the power of AI, you can create passive income streams that work for you around the clock.

One of the key principles of passive income is leveraging your time and resources to generate income without constantly trading your time for money. With AI-driven online businesses, you can create automated systems that generate income even while you sleep. By utilizing AI algorithms to analyze data, predict trends, and optimize processes, you can create passive income streams that require minimal maintenance and yield maximum returns.

Monetizing AI-generated content is another powerful way to create passive income. By leveraging AI to create high-quality content, such as articles, videos, and social media posts, you can attract a steady stream of traffic and generate income through advertising, affiliate marketing, and sponsored content. With AI's ability to analyze audience behavior and preferences, you can tailor your content to maximize engagement and conversions, leading to a steady flow of passive income.

When it comes to creating passive income streams with AI, it's essential to choose the right tools and platforms that align with your goals and expertise. Whether you're a seasoned entrepreneur or a beginner looking to dip your toes into the world of passive income, there are plenty of AI-powered tools and platforms available to help you get started. From AI-driven content creation tools to automated marketing platforms, the possibilities are endless when it comes to harnessing AI for financial freedom.

In conclusion, understanding the basics of passive income and how artificial intelligence can help you generate wealth is essential for anyone looking to make money with passive income in today's digital age. By leveraging AI to create automated systems, monetize content, and optimize processes, you can create passive income streams that work for you, allowing you to achieve financial freedom and live life on your terms. So, if you're ready to take control of your financial future and harness the power of AI for passive income, this subchapter is the perfect starting point for your journey to financial success.

Introduction to Artificial Intelligence

Welcome to the world of artificial intelligence (AI) and passive income. In this subchapter, we will explore the basics of artificial intelligence and how you can harness its power to achieve financial freedom. Whether you are interested in creating passive income streams with AI-driven online businesses or monetizing AI-generated content for passive income, this subchapter will provide you with the knowledge and tools you need to succeed in the rapidly evolving digital landscape.

Artificial intelligence is a branch of computer science that focuses on the development of intelligent machines that can perform tasks typically requiring human intelligence, such as visual perception, speech recognition, decision-making, and language translation. AI technologies have revolutionized industries ranging from healthcare to finance, and have the potential to transform how we work, live, and interact with technology in the future.

For people that want to make money with Passive Income How to Make Money with Artificial Intelligence, AI presents a unique opportunity to automate and optimize business processes, streamline operations, and drive growth. By leveraging AI technologies such as machine learning, natural language processing, and computer vision, entrepreneurs can create innovative products and services that cater to changing consumer preferences and market demands.

Creating passive income streams with AI-driven online businesses is a lucrative way to generate wealth and achieve financial independence. From chatbots and virtual assistants to personalized product recommendations and predictive analytics, AI-powered solutions can help businesses attract and retain customers, increase sales and profitability, and gain a competitive edge in the marketplace.

Monetizing AI-generated content for passive income is another promising avenue for entrepreneurs looking to diversify their revenue streams and build long-term wealth. Whether you are a content creator, influencer, or e-commerce store owner, AI technologies can help you create high-quality, engaging content that resonates with your target audience, drives traffic and conversions, and generates passive income through advertising, affiliate marketing, and sponsored partnerships.

The Intersection of Passive Income and AI

The intersection of passive income and artificial intelligence (AI) is a powerful and rapidly evolving field that offers exciting opportunities for individuals looking to make money without having to actively work for it. AI technology has revolutionized the way we do business, allowing for the automation of tasks that were once time-consuming and labor-intensive. This has opened up new possibilities for creating passive income streams through AI-driven online businesses.

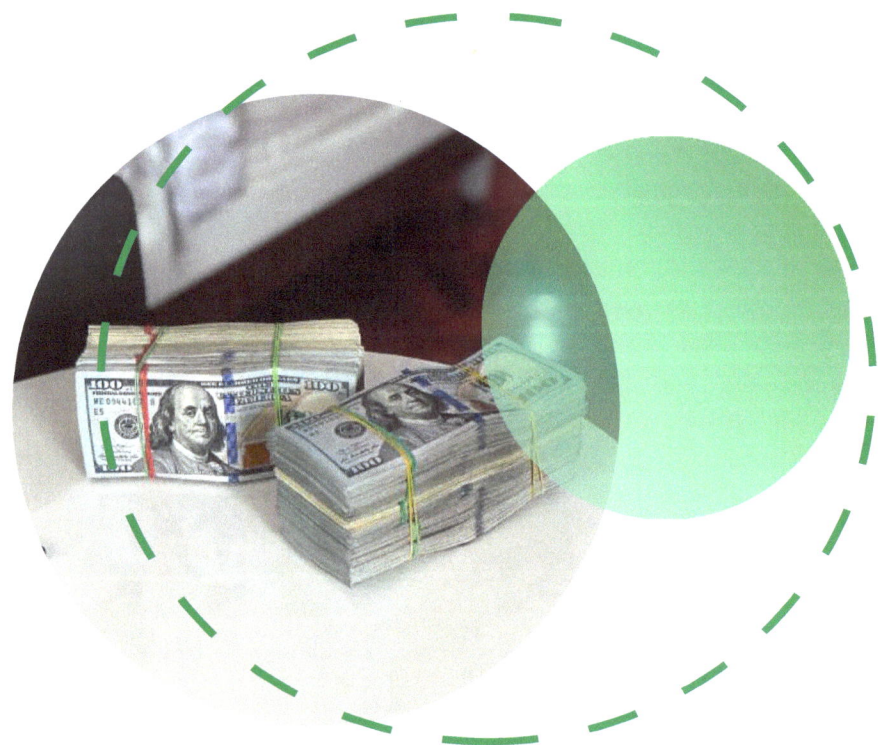

One of the key ways in which AI can be used to generate passive income is through the creation of AI-driven online businesses. These businesses leverage AI technology to automate processes such as customer service, marketing, and sales, allowing for the creation of scalable and profitable ventures that require minimal ongoing maintenance. By harnessing the power of AI, entrepreneurs can build online businesses that generate passive income streams while they focus on other aspects of their lives. Another way in which AI can be used to generate passive income is through the monetization of AI-generated content. AI technology has advanced to the point where it can create high-quality written and visual content that is indistinguishable from human-generated content. This opens up new opportunities for individuals to generate passive income by creating and selling AI-generated content through platforms such as blogs, websites, and social media channels.

For individuals looking to make money with passive income through AI, it is important to understand the potential risks and challenges associated with this field. While AI technology offers immense opportunities for creating passive income streams, it also comes with its own set of challenges, such as data privacy concerns, ethical implications, and the risk of job displacement. It is important for individuals to stay informed about the latest developments in AI technology and to carefully consider the potential risks and rewards before diving into this field.

Overall, the intersection of passive income and AI offers exciting opportunities for individuals looking to make money without having to actively work for it. By harnessing the power of AI technology, entrepreneurs can create scalable and profitable online businesses, monetize AI-generated content, and build passive income streams that provide financial freedom and flexibility. With careful planning and strategic decision-making, individuals can leverage AI technology to create sustainable passive income streams that allow them to achieve their financial goals and live the lifestyle of their dreams.

02

Chapter 2: Leveraging AI for Passive Income

AI-driven Online Businesses

In today's digital age, the possibilities for creating passive income streams with AI-driven online businesses are endless. Artificial Intelligence (AI) has revolutionized the way we do business, allowing entrepreneurs to automate processes, analyze data, and generate content with unprecedented speed and accuracy. For people that want to make money with Passive Income How to Make Money with Artificial Intelligence, harnessing the power of AI is essential to staying ahead of the competition and maximizing profits.

One of the most popular ways to monetize AI-generated content for passive income is through affiliate marketing. By using AI algorithms to analyze customer behavior and preferences, online businesses can target their marketing efforts more effectively, increasing the likelihood of conversions and earning passive income through affiliate commissions. With AI-driven online businesses, entrepreneurs can leverage the power of machine learning and predictive analytics to optimize their marketing strategies and drive sales on autopilot.

Another lucrative opportunity for creating passive income streams with AI-driven online businesses is through e-commerce platforms. By using AI algorithms to personalize product recommendations, optimize pricing strategies, and streamline the customer shopping experience, online retailers can increase sales and generate passive income with minimal effort. With the right AI tools and strategies in place, entrepreneurs can scale their e-commerce businesses quickly and efficiently, reaching a global audience and maximizing their profits.

For entrepreneurs looking to diversify their passive income streams, AI-driven online businesses offer a wealth of opportunities. From content creation and social media marketing to customer service and data analysis, AI technologies can automate a wide range of tasks, freeing up time and resources to focus on growing your business. By leveraging the power of AI, entrepreneurs can build scalable online businesses that generate passive income 24/7, allowing them to achieve financial freedom and live life on their own terms.

In conclusion, for people that want to make money with Passive Income How to Make Money with Artificial Intelligence, creating passive income streams with AI-driven online businesses is a smart and strategic investment. By harnessing the power of AI technologies, entrepreneurs can automate processes, optimize marketing strategies, and generate content with unprecedented speed and accuracy, allowing them to scale their businesses quickly and efficiently. With the right tools and strategies in place, online entrepreneurs can maximize their profits, achieve financial freedom, and create a sustainable source of passive income for years to come.

Automating Passive Income Streams with AI

In today's rapidly advancing technological landscape, the concept of passive income has taken on a whole new level with the integration of artificial intelligence (AI). With the rise of AI-driven online businesses and platforms, individuals now have the opportunity to automate their passive income streams like never before. In this subchapter, we will explore how you can harness the power of AI to create sustainable and profitable passive income streams.

One of the key ways in which AI can be used to automate passive income streams is through the creation of AI-driven online businesses. By leveraging AI algorithms and machine learning technology, individuals can create online platforms that generate income on autopilot. These businesses can range from e-commerce stores that utilize AI-powered product recommendations to content websites that use AI to personalize user experiences and drive ad revenue.

Another way to automate passive income streams with AI is by monetizing AI-generated content. With the advancements in natural language processing and content generation algorithms, individuals can create and distribute AI-generated content that attracts a wide audience and generates passive income through advertising, affiliate marketing, or subscription models. By leveraging AI to create high-quality and engaging content at scale, individuals can build a sustainable passive income stream that requires minimal ongoing effort.

Furthermore, AI can also be used to optimize and streamline existing passive income streams. By using AI-powered tools and analytics platforms, individuals can track and analyze the performance of their passive income sources in real-time, identify areas for improvement, and implement automated solutions to maximize revenue and minimize costs. This level of automation and optimization can help individuals achieve financial freedom and create a truly passive income stream that grows and evolves over time. In conclusion, the integration of AI into passive income strategies has opened up new opportunities for individuals to create sustainable and profitable income streams with minimal effort. By leveraging AI-driven online businesses, monetizing AI-generated content, and optimizing existing passive income streams with AI-powered tools, individuals can harness the power of artificial intelligence to achieve financial freedom and create a truly passive income stream that generates income on autopilot. With the right mindset and strategies, anyone can tap into the potential of AI for passive income and build a successful and lucrative online business.

In this subchapter, we will explore some of the most powerful tools and resources available for those looking to harness the power of artificial intelligence for passive income generation. With the right tools at your disposal, you can streamline your processes, maximize your efficiency, and ultimately increase your earnings in the world of AI-driven passive income.

Tools and Resources for AI-driven Passive Income

One essential tool for anyone looking to make money with AI-driven passive income is a reliable data analytics platform. By utilizing advanced data analytics tools, you can gain valuable insights into customer behavior, market trends, and other key metrics that can help you optimize your passive income streams. Platforms like Google Analytics, IBM Watson, and Tableau are just a few examples of the many powerful tools available for data analysis.

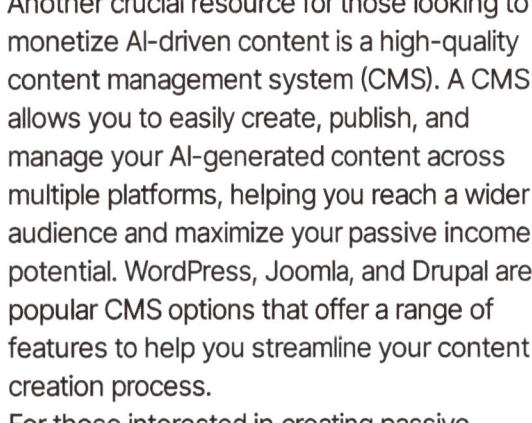

Another crucial resource for those looking to monetize AI-driven content is a high-quality content management system (CMS). A CMS allows you to easily create, publish, and manage your AI-generated content across multiple platforms, helping you reach a wider audience and maximize your passive income potential. WordPress, Joomla, and Drupal are popular CMS options that offer a range of features to help you streamline your content creation process.

For those interested in creating passive income streams with AI-driven online businesses, a reliable e-commerce platform is essential. Platforms like Shopify, WooCommerce, and Magento offer powerful features such as automated product recommendations, personalized shopping experiences, and seamless payment processing, making it easier than ever to monetize your AI-generated products and services.

In conclusion, the world of AI-driven passive income offers endless opportunities for those willing to invest the time and effort into leveraging the power of artificial intelligence. By utilizing the right tools and resources, you can optimize your passive income streams, increase your earnings, and ultimately achieve financial freedom through the power of AI. With the right mindset and dedication, anyone can unlock the potential of AI-driven passive income and build a successful online business that generates passive income for years to come.

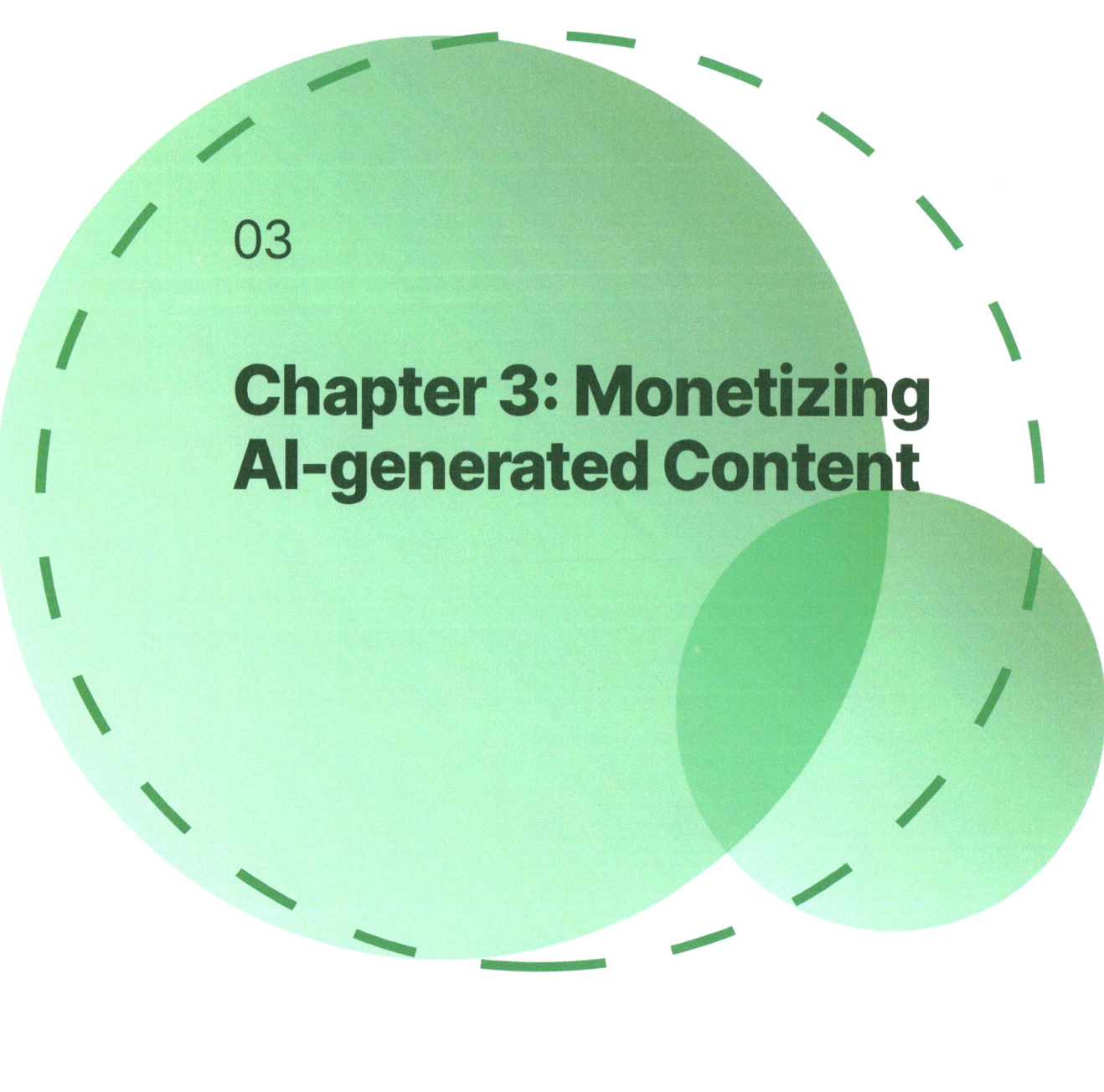

03

Chapter 3: Monetizing AI-generated Content

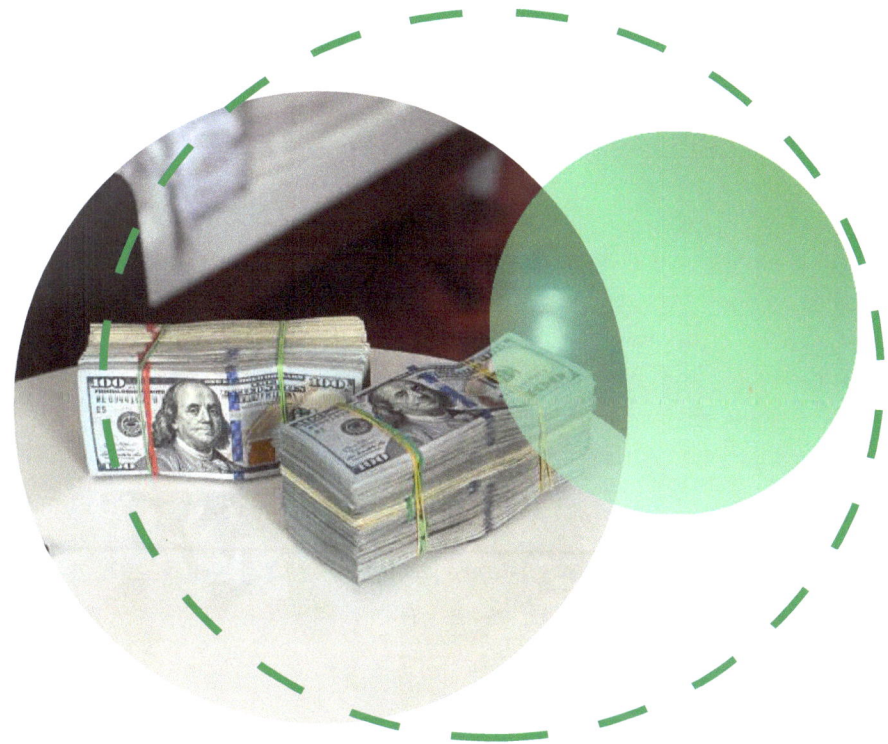

Creating AI-generated Content for Passive Income

Creating AI-generated content for passive income is a lucrative opportunity for those looking to harness the power of artificial intelligence to generate income. With the rise of AI technology, creating content has become more accessible and efficient than ever before. By utilizing AI tools and platforms, individuals can create high-quality, engaging content in a fraction of the time it would take to do so manually.

One of the key benefits of creating AI-generated content for passive income is the ability to scale your efforts. With AI tools, you can quickly and easily create a large volume of content across various platforms, reaching a wider audience and increasing your potential for monetization. This scalability allows you to generate passive income streams from multiple sources, maximizing your earning potential.

In addition to scalability, AI-generated content also offers the advantage of customization. AI tools can analyze data and user behavior to create personalized content that resonates with your target audience. By tailoring your content to meet the specific needs and interests of your audience, you can increase engagement and conversion rates, ultimately leading to higher passive income earnings.

Another benefit of creating AI-generated content for passive income is the ability to automate the content creation process. By setting up AI algorithms to generate content on a regular basis, you can free up your time to focus on other aspects of your business or personal life. This automation allows you to generate passive income streams consistently without having to constantly monitor or update your content.

Overall, creating AI-generated content for passive income is a smart investment for those looking to monetize their online presence. By leveraging AI technology to create high-quality, engaging content, you can scale your efforts, customize your content to meet the needs of your audience, and automate the content creation process. With the right tools and strategies in place, you can harness the power of AI to generate passive income streams and achieve financial freedom.

Marketing Strategies for AI-generated Content

In today's digital age, artificial intelligence (AI) has revolutionized the way we create and consume content. With the rise of AI-generated content, individuals have found new opportunities to make money through passive income streams. In this subchapter, we will explore the various marketing strategies that can be utilized to maximize the potential of AI-generated content and generate a steady stream of revenue.

One of the key marketing strategies for AI-generated content is to leverage social media platforms. With the vast reach and engagement opportunities that platforms like Facebook, Instagram, and Twitter offer, creators can promote their AI-generated content to a wider audience. By using targeted advertising and engaging with followers, creators can drive traffic to their content and increase their passive income potential.

Another effective marketing strategy for AI-generated content is search engine optimization (SEO). By optimizing content with relevant keywords and meta tags, creators can improve their visibility on search engine results pages. This can lead to increased organic traffic, higher click-through rates, and ultimately, more revenue generated from their AI-driven online businesses.

Email marketing is also a powerful tool for promoting AI-generated content. By building an email list of subscribers who are interested in the content being produced, creators can send targeted campaigns to drive traffic and increase engagement. This direct communication with the audience can lead to higher conversion rates and ultimately, more passive income generated from monetizing AI-generated content. Additionally, collaborations with influencers and other content creators can help expand the reach of AI-generated content. By partnering with individuals who have a larger following, creators can tap into new audiences and increase their passive income potential. This strategy can be particularly effective for creators looking to monetize their AI-generated content through sponsored content or affiliate marketing partnerships.

Overall, by implementing a combination of social media marketing, SEO, email marketing, and influencer collaborations, creators can effectively market their AI-generated content and maximize their passive income potential. With the right strategies in place, individuals can harness the power of AI to create sustainable revenue streams and achieve financial freedom.

Maximizing Revenue from AI-generated Content

In the digital age, AI-generated content has become a powerful tool for maximizing revenue and creating passive income streams. By harnessing the power of artificial intelligence, individuals can create high-quality content at a fraction of the time and cost of traditional methods. This subchapter will explore the various ways in which individuals can leverage AI-generated content to generate passive income and maximize their revenue potential.

One of the key strategies for maximizing revenue from AI-generated content is to focus on niche markets. By targeting specific niches with high demand and low competition, individuals can create content that is highly sought after by consumers. This can lead to increased traffic, engagement, and ultimately, revenue. By using AI to identify profitable niches and create tailored content, individuals can position themselves as leaders in their respective industries and maximize their earning potential.

Another important aspect of maximizing revenue from AI-generated content is to optimize for search engines. By using AI algorithms to analyze keywords, trends, and user behavior, individuals can create content that is highly optimized for search engines. This can lead to increased visibility, higher rankings, and ultimately, more traffic and revenue. By continuously monitoring and adjusting their content strategy based on AI insights, individuals can stay ahead of the competition and maximize their revenue potential.

Furthermore, individuals can monetize their AI-generated content through various channels, such as affiliate marketing, sponsored content, and advertising. By partnering with brands and companies that align with their niche and target audience, individuals can generate passive income through partnerships and collaborations. By leveraging AI to analyze consumer behavior and preferences, individuals can create content that resonates with their audience and drives conversions. This can lead to increased revenue and long-term success in the competitive online marketplace.

Overall, maximizing revenue from AI-generated content requires a strategic approach and a deep understanding of the digital landscape. By focusing on niche markets, optimizing for search engines, and monetizing through various channels, individuals can create passive income streams and achieve financial freedom. With the right tools, techniques, and mindset, anyone can harness the power of artificial intelligence to create a successful online business and generate sustainable revenue for years to come.

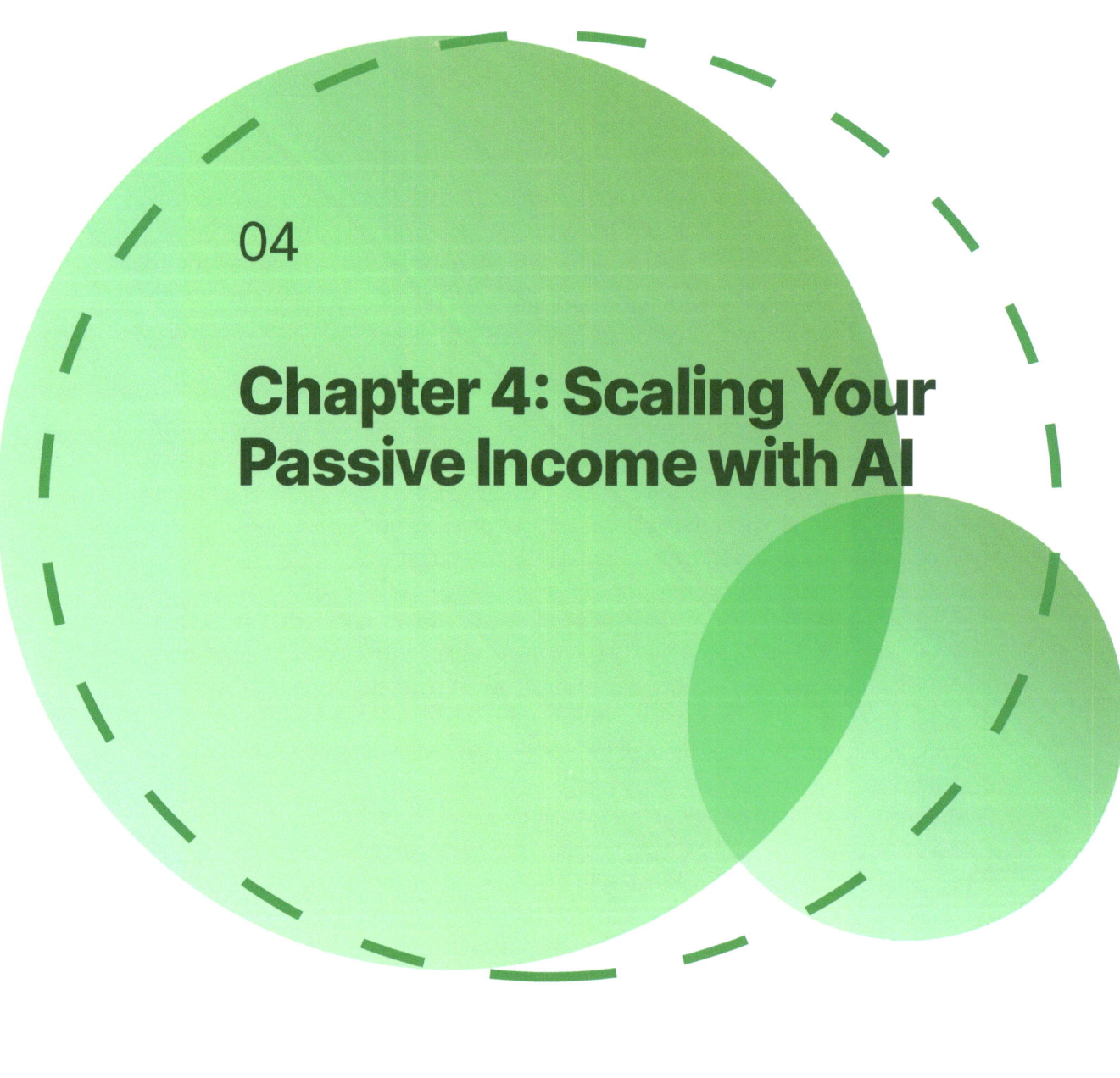

04

Chapter 4: Scaling Your Passive Income with AI

Building a Passive Income Portfolio with AI

In today's fast-paced world, the concept of passive income has become increasingly popular among individuals who are looking to make money without actively working for it. One innovative way to build a passive income portfolio is by harnessing the power of artificial intelligence (AI). By leveraging AI technology, individuals can create passive income streams that generate revenue on autopilot. This subchapter will explore the various ways in which AI can be used to build a passive income portfolio and provide tips on how to effectively utilize this cutting-edge technology.

One of the most common ways to build a passive income portfolio with AI is through AI-driven online businesses. These businesses utilize AI algorithms to automate processes such as customer service, marketing, and product recommendations. By leveraging AI technology, individuals can create online businesses that require minimal human intervention, allowing them to generate passive income without having to actively manage the day-to-day operations of the business. This subchapter will provide tips on how to set up and scale an AI-driven online business to maximize passive income potential.

Another way to build a passive income portfolio with AI is by monetizing AI-generated content. AI algorithms can be used to generate content such as articles, videos, and social media posts that can be monetized through advertising, affiliate marketing, and sponsored content. By leveraging AI technology to create high-quality, engaging content, individuals can attract a larger audience and generate passive income through various monetization channels. This subchapter will provide strategies on how to create AI-generated content that resonates with audiences and drives passive income.

In addition to AI-driven online businesses and AI-generated content, individuals can also build a passive income portfolio by investing in AI-powered financial tools and platforms. These tools utilize AI algorithms to analyze market trends, predict investment opportunities, and optimize investment portfolios. By leveraging AI technology in their investment strategies, individuals can generate passive income through dividends, interest, and capital gains. This subchapter will explore the various AI-powered financial tools available to investors and provide tips on how to use them to build a passive income portfolio.

Overall, building a passive income portfolio with AI requires a strategic approach and a willingness to embrace cutting-edge technology. By leveraging AI-driven online businesses, AI-generated content, and AI-powered financial tools, individuals can create passive income streams that generate revenue on autopilot. This subchapter will provide insights and strategies on how to effectively harness the power of AI to build a successful passive income portfolio and achieve financial freedom.

Scaling Your AI-driven Passive Income Streams

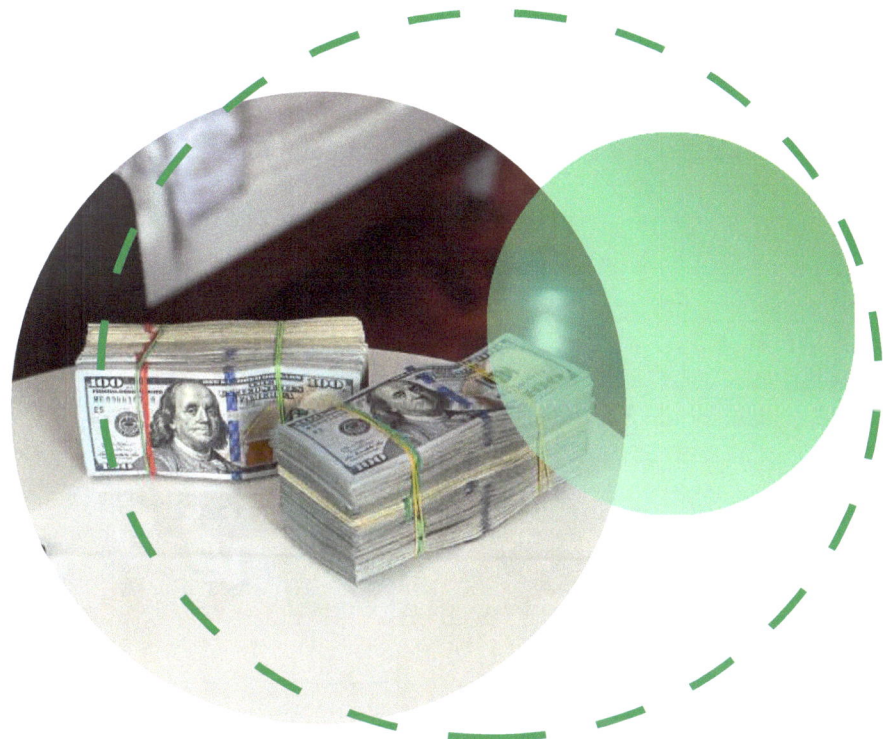

In the subchapter "Scaling Your AI-driven Passive Income Streams," we will explore strategies for maximizing the potential of your AI-powered online businesses to generate passive income. As technology continues to advance, leveraging artificial intelligence has become a game-changer for entrepreneurs looking to create sustainable passive income streams. By harnessing the power of AI, you can automate and optimize various aspects of your online business, allowing you to scale your operations and increase your revenue potential.

One of the key ways to scale your AI-driven passive income streams is to continuously refine and improve your AI algorithms. By collecting and analyzing data generated by your AI systems, you can identify areas for optimization and enhancement. This iterative process of refinement will not only improve the performance of your AI systems but also enable you to stay ahead of the competition in your niche. By constantly fine-tuning your AI algorithms, you can ensure that your passive income streams continue to grow and evolve over time.

Another effective strategy for scaling your AI-driven passive income streams is to diversify your revenue sources. While your primary focus may be on a specific AI-driven online business, it is important to explore opportunities to monetize AI-generated content in other ways. For example, you could license your AI algorithms to other businesses or sell AI-generated products and services to a wider audience. By diversifying your revenue sources, you can create multiple streams of passive income that complement and support each other, ultimately increasing your overall profitability.

In addition to refining your AI algorithms and diversifying your revenue sources, scaling your AI-driven passive income streams also requires a strategic approach to marketing and promotion. By leveraging AI-powered tools and analytics, you can identify and target the most profitable market segments for your products and services. This targeted marketing approach will not only help you attract more customers but also increase your conversion rates and maximize your revenue potential. By investing in AI-driven marketing strategies, you can scale your passive income streams more effectively and efficiently.

Ultimately, scaling your AI-driven passive income streams requires a combination of ongoing refinement, diversification, and strategic marketing. By continuously improving your AI algorithms, exploring new revenue sources, and targeting the right market segments, you can maximize the potential of your online businesses and create sustainable passive income streams. With the right approach and mindset, you can harness the power of AI to achieve financial freedom and build a successful online business that generates passive income for years to come.

Long-term Strategies for Financial Freedom

In order to achieve financial freedom through passive income, it is essential to develop long-term strategies that leverage the power of artificial intelligence. By harnessing AI technology, individuals can create sustainable income streams that require minimal effort to maintain. In this subchapter, we will explore some key strategies for using AI to build wealth over the long term. One effective long-term strategy for financial freedom is to create AI-driven online businesses that generate passive income. By leveraging AI algorithms to automate tasks and optimize processes, entrepreneurs can build scalable online ventures that continue to generate revenue without constant oversight. This can include e-commerce platforms, affiliate marketing websites, or digital content marketplaces that utilize AI to personalize user experiences and maximize profits.

Another key strategy for long-term financial freedom is to monetize AI-generated content for passive income. This can involve creating and selling digital products or services that are powered by AI technology, such as ebooks, online courses, or software applications. By leveraging AI to create high-quality and in-demand content, individuals can attract a steady stream of customers and generate passive income over time.

One important aspect of long-term financial freedom is diversification. By spreading investments and income streams across different AI-driven opportunities, individuals can reduce risk and increase their chances of long-term success. This can involve investing in multiple AI-driven online businesses, content creation projects, or AI-powered investment platforms to build a diverse portfolio of passive income sources.

In conclusion, achieving financial freedom through passive income requires a long-term perspective and strategic use of AI technology. By creating AI-driven online businesses, monetizing AI-generated content, and diversifying income streams, individuals can build wealth over time and secure their financial future. With the right approach and a commitment to long-term success, anyone can harness the power of AI for financial freedom.

05

Chapter 5: Overcoming Challenges and Pitfalls

Common Pitfalls in AI-driven Passive Income

In the world of passive income, harnessing the power of artificial intelligence (AI) can be a game-changer. AI-driven passive income streams have the potential to generate significant wealth with minimal effort. However, there are common pitfalls that individuals must be aware of in order to avoid costly mistakes and maximize their earnings. In this subchapter, we will explore some of the most common pitfalls in AI-driven passive income and provide strategies for success.

One common pitfall in AI-driven passive income is relying too heavily on automation. While AI can streamline processes and increase efficiency, it is important to remember that human oversight is still necessary. Over-automation can lead to errors and oversights that can negatively impact your passive income streams. It is essential to strike a balance between automation and human supervision to ensure the success of your AI-driven passive income ventures.

Another common pitfall in AI-driven passive income is failing to adapt to changing market conditions. AI algorithms are constantly evolving, and what works today may not work tomorrow. It is crucial to stay informed about market trends and be willing to pivot your strategies as needed. Failing to adapt can result in missed opportunities and decreased passive income earnings. By staying proactive and flexible, you can position yourself for long-term success in the world of AI-driven passive income.

One of the most common pitfalls in AI-driven passive income is underestimating the importance of quality content. In the digital age, content is king, and AI-generated content is no exception. It is essential to provide valuable and engaging content to attract and retain customers. Failing to prioritize content quality can lead to decreased traffic, lower conversion rates, and ultimately, reduced passive income earnings. By focusing on creating high-quality content, you can set yourself apart from the competition and build a loyal customer base for your AI-driven passive income streams.

Another common pitfall in AI-driven passive income is neglecting to diversify your income streams. Relying on a single source of passive income leaves you vulnerable to market fluctuations and changes in consumer behavior. By diversifying your income streams and exploring multiple AI-driven opportunities, you can spread your risk and increase your earning potential. Diversification can also provide stability and security in uncertain economic times, ensuring that you have multiple streams of passive income to rely on.

In conclusion, while AI-driven passive income has the potential to revolutionize your financial future, there are common pitfalls that must be avoided in order to succeed. By maintaining a balance between automation and human oversight, adapting to changing market conditions, prioritizing quality content, and diversifying your income streams, you can maximize your earnings and build a sustainable passive income empire. With careful planning and strategic execution, you can harness the power of AI to achieve financial freedom and create the life of your dreams.

Strategies for Overcoming Challenges

In the world of passive income, challenges are inevitable. Whether you are just starting out or have been in the game for a while, there will always be obstacles to overcome. However, with the right strategies in place, you can navigate these challenges and continue on your path to financial freedom. In this subchapter, we will discuss some key strategies for overcoming the hurdles that may come your way as you harness the power of artificial intelligence to generate passive income.

One of the most important strategies for overcoming challenges in the world of passive income is to stay adaptable. The landscape of AI-driven online businesses is constantly changing, and what works today may not work tomorrow. By remaining flexible and open to new ideas and technologies, you can pivot when necessary and stay ahead of the curve.

Another crucial strategy for overcoming challenges is to stay focused on your goals. It can be easy to get discouraged when faced with setbacks or obstacles, but by keeping your eye on the prize and reminding yourself of why you started on this journey in the first place, you can stay motivated and push through even the toughest challenges.

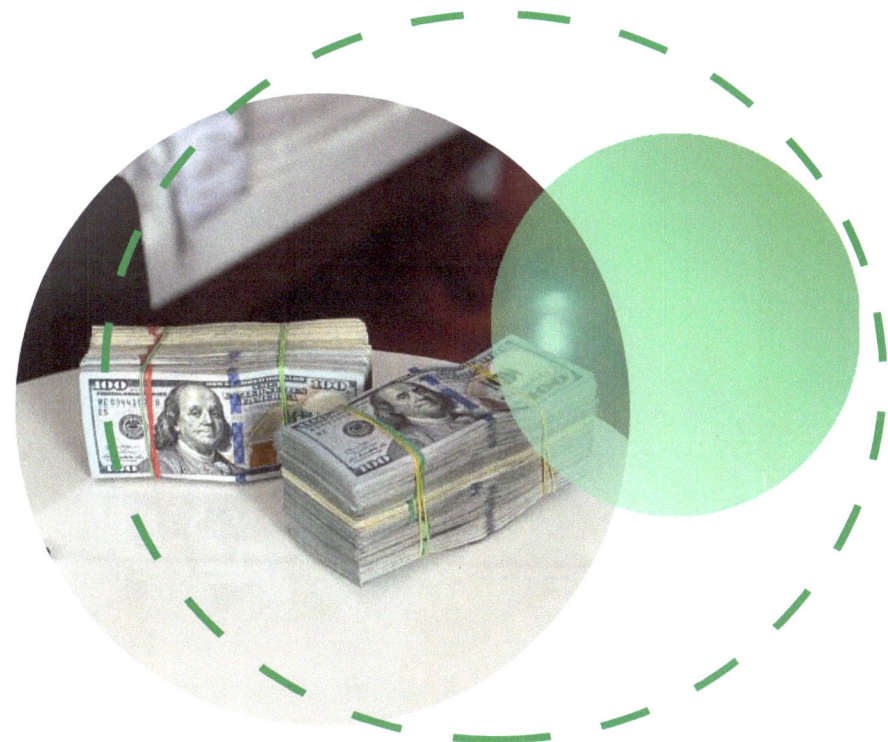

Additionally, building a strong support network can be instrumental in overcoming challenges in the world of passive income. Surround yourself with like-minded individuals who can offer advice, support, and encouragement when you need it most. By leveraging the collective knowledge and experience of others, you can navigate challenges more effectively and come out on top.

In the realm of monetizing AI-generated content for passive income, it is also important to continually educate yourself and stay informed about the latest trends and developments in the industry. By staying on top of emerging technologies and strategies, you can position yourself as a leader in your niche and stay one step ahead of the competition.

Finally, remember that challenges are a natural part of any entrepreneurial journey. By viewing obstacles as opportunities for growth and learning, you can turn setbacks into stepping stones towards success. With the right mindset, strategies, and support network in place, you can overcome any challenge that comes your way and continue on your path to financial freedom through passive income and artificial intelligence.

Maintaining Passive Income Sustainability

In order to maintain passive income sustainability in your AI-driven online business, it's important to continuously evaluate and optimize your revenue streams. This means keeping a close eye on your key performance indicators, such as conversion rates, customer retention, and overall profitability. By regularly monitoring these metrics, you can identify areas for improvement and make informed decisions to maximize your passive income potential.

Another key aspect of maintaining passive income sustainability is diversifying your revenue streams. Relying on a single source of income leaves you vulnerable to fluctuations in the market or changes in consumer behavior. By diversifying your revenue streams through multiple AI-driven online businesses or monetizing AI-generated content across different platforms, you can create a more stable and resilient passive income portfolio.

Consistent and high-quality content creation is essential for maintaining passive income sustainability. In the world of AI-driven online businesses, content is king. By consistently producing valuable and engaging content, you can attract and retain a loyal audience, drive traffic to your online platforms, and ultimately increase your passive income potential. Leveraging AI technology to generate and optimize content can help streamline your content creation process and ensure that your content remains relevant and competitive in the market.

Building a strong brand and reputation is crucial for maintaining passive income sustainability in the long run. By delivering exceptional products or services, providing top-notch customer support, and building a strong online presence, you can establish trust and credibility with your audience. A strong brand and reputation not only attract more customers and clients but also help you retain existing ones, ultimately leading to a more stable and sustainable passive income stream.

Lastly, staying informed and adapting to changes in the AI and passive income landscape is key to maintaining sustainability. The world of AI and passive income is constantly evolving, with new technologies, platforms, and opportunities emerging all the time. By staying up-to-date with the latest trends and developments in the industry, you can position yourself as a leader in your niche and capitalize on new opportunities to grow your passive income streams. Embracing change and innovation will help you stay ahead of the curve and maintain a successful and sustainable passive income business in the long term.

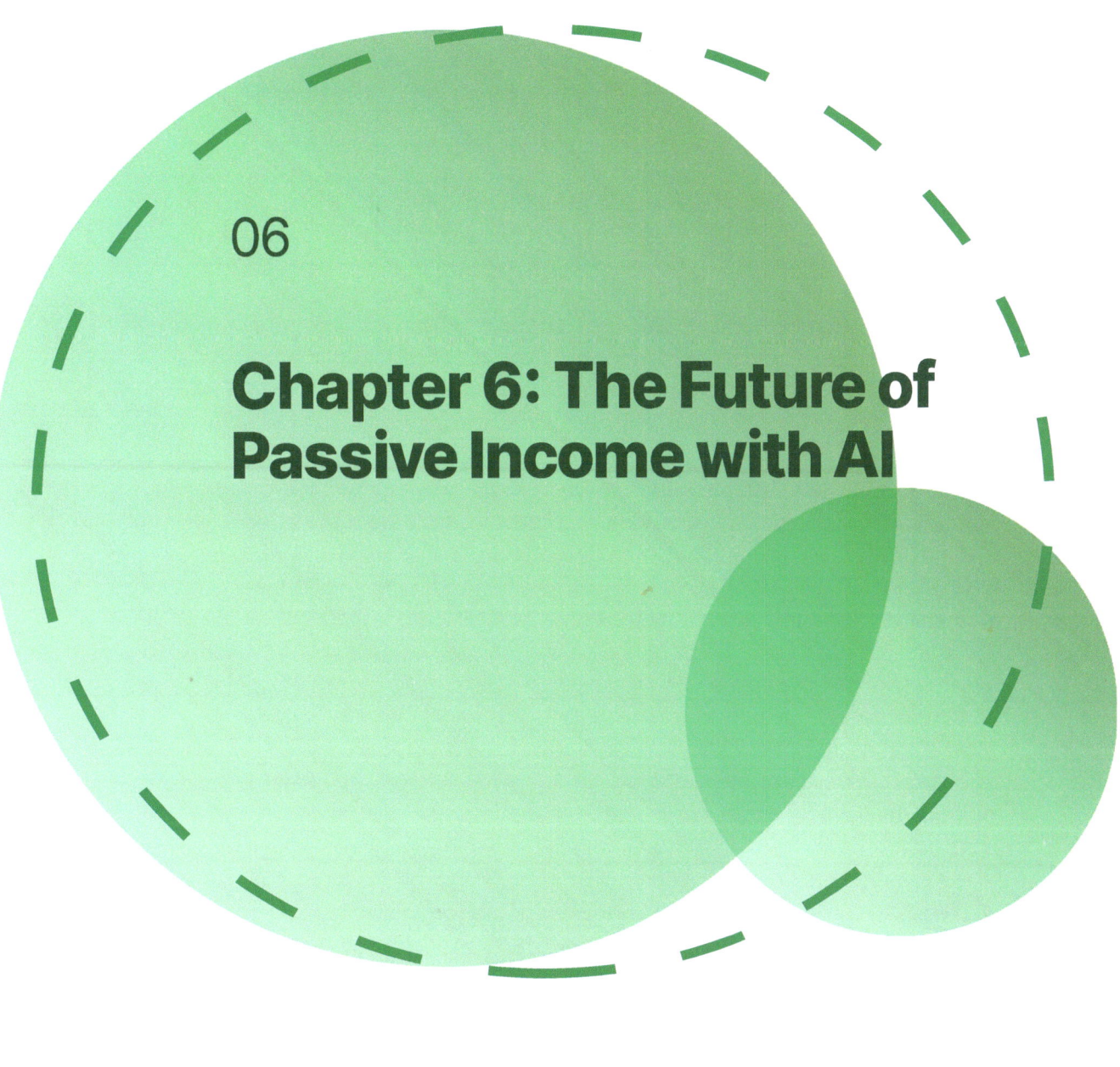

06

Chapter 6: The Future of Passive Income with AI

Trends and Innovations in AI-driven Passive Income

In recent years, the intersection of artificial intelligence (AI) and passive income has created a wealth of opportunities for individuals looking to make money without actively working. This subchapter, "Trends and Innovations in AI-driven Passive Income," explores the latest developments in harnessing AI for financial freedom.

One of the most notable trends in AI-driven passive income is the rise of AI-powered online businesses. From automated e-commerce stores to AI-driven marketing campaigns, entrepreneurs are leveraging AI technology to streamline operations and maximize profits. By utilizing AI algorithms to analyze data and predict consumer behavior, online businesses can optimize their strategies for success.

Another key trend in AI-driven passive income is the monetization of AI-generated content. With advancements in natural language processing and image recognition, AI can now create high-quality written and visual content at scale. This content can be monetized through various channels, such as affiliate marketing, advertising, and sponsored content. By automating the content creation process, individuals can generate passive income without the need for constant supervision.

Furthermore, the integration of AI into investment strategies has revolutionized passive income generation. AI-powered robo-advisors and trading algorithms can analyze market trends and make investment decisions on behalf of investors. This hands-off approach to investing allows individuals to earn passive income from their investments without the need for extensive financial knowledge or time-consuming research.

In conclusion, the trends and innovations in AI-driven passive income are transforming the way individuals make money online. By capitalizing on AI technology in online businesses, content creation, and investment strategies, individuals can create sustainable passive income streams that require minimal effort to maintain. As AI continues to evolve, the opportunities for passive income generation will only continue to expand, making it an exciting time for those looking to achieve financial freedom through AI-driven strategies.

Opportunities for Growth and Expansion

In this subchapter, we will explore the various opportunities for growth and expansion in the realm of passive income through artificial intelligence (AI). As technology continues to advance at a rapid pace, there are more opportunities than ever before to harness the power of AI for financial freedom. Whether you are interested in creating passive income streams with AI-driven online businesses or monetizing AI-generated content, there are numerous ways to capitalize on this growing trend.

One of the key opportunities for growth and expansion in the world of passive income with AI is through the creation of online businesses that are driven by artificial intelligence. From e-commerce platforms to digital marketing agencies, there are countless ways to leverage AI technology to streamline operations, improve efficiency, and ultimately increase profitability. By incorporating AI into your business model, you can automate tasks, analyze data, and optimize processes to maximize your earning potential.

Another lucrative opportunity for growth and expansion in the realm of passive income with AI is through the creation of AI-generated content. From blog posts and social media updates to videos and podcasts, there are endless possibilities for monetizing content that is created or enhanced by artificial intelligence. By leveraging AI tools and platforms, you can create high-quality, engaging content that resonates with your target audience and drives traffic to your website or online store.

For those looking to capitalize on the growing trend of passive income with AI, there are also opportunities to invest in AI-driven startups and technologies. By staying informed about the latest developments in the AI space, you can identify promising opportunities for investment and growth. Whether you choose to invest in AI-powered financial services, healthcare solutions, or marketing platforms, there are numerous ways to profit from the rapid advancements in artificial intelligence.

In conclusion, the opportunities for growth and expansion in the realm of passive income with AI are vast and diverse. Whether you are interested in creating passive income streams with AI-driven online businesses, monetizing AI-generated content, or investing in AI-driven startups, there are countless ways to harness the power of artificial intelligence for financial freedom. By staying informed, exploring new opportunities, and taking calculated risks, you can position yourself for success in this exciting and rapidly evolving field.

The Future Outlook for Financial Freedom

The future outlook for financial freedom is bright for those who harness the power of artificial intelligence (AI) to create passive income streams. With advancements in technology and the increasing demand for AI-driven solutions, there are countless opportunities for individuals to generate wealth without the need for constant effort or active participation. By leveraging AI, people can create online businesses that run on autopilot, generate passive income, and provide financial security for the future.

One of the key strategies for achieving financial freedom through AI is to create passive income streams with AI-driven online businesses. These businesses can be set up to run automatically, using algorithms and machine learning to optimize processes, analyze data, and make informed decisions. By leveraging AI technology, individuals can create scalable and profitable online ventures that generate income without the need for constant supervision or manual labor. This allows for greater flexibility, time freedom, and the potential for exponential growth in income.

Another avenue for achieving financial freedom through AI is by monetizing AI-generated content for passive income. With the rise of content creation tools powered by AI, individuals can create high-quality, engaging content at scale without the need for specialized skills or expertise. By monetizing this content through various platforms such as YouTube, podcasts, blogs, or social media, individuals can generate passive income streams that grow over time. This passive income can provide financial stability, independence, and the freedom to pursue other interests or investments.

As the demand for AI-driven solutions continues to grow, the opportunities for creating passive income with AI will only increase. By staying informed about the latest AI trends, technologies, and tools, individuals can position themselves to capitalize on these opportunities and achieve financial freedom. Whether through online businesses, content creation, or other AI-driven ventures, the future outlook for financial freedom is promising for those who are willing to invest the time and effort to harness the power of AI.

In conclusion, the future outlook for financial freedom through AI is bright for those who are willing to take advantage of the opportunities available. By creating passive income streams with AI-driven online businesses, monetizing AI-generated content, and staying informed about the latest AI trends, individuals can achieve financial security, independence, and the freedom to live life on their own terms. With the right strategies and mindset, anyone can harness the power of AI to create a path to financial freedom and achieve their goals.

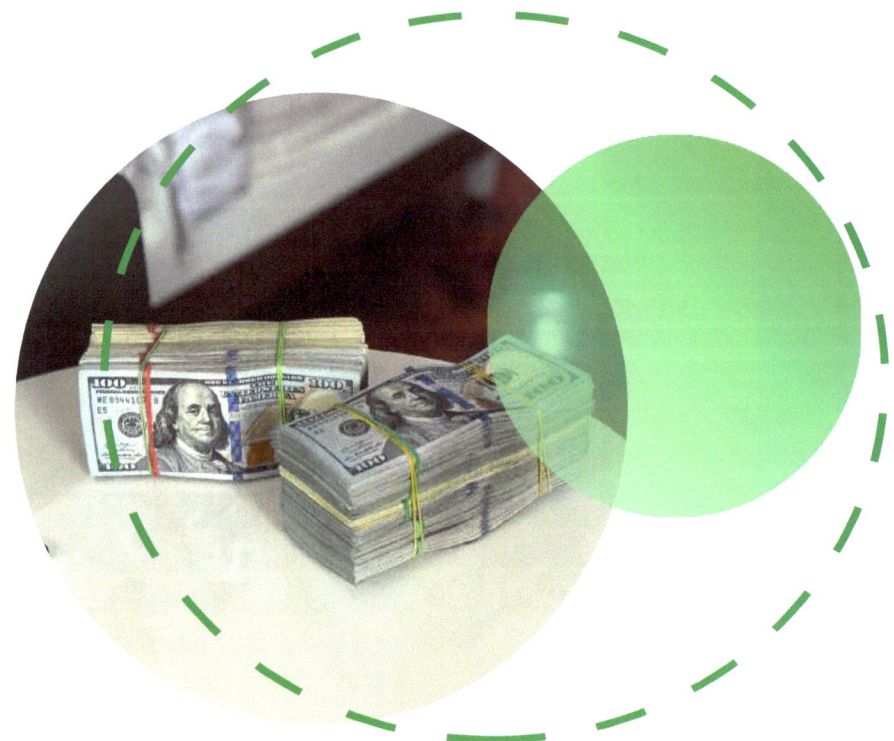